Natural Selections

Winner of the Iowa Poetry Prize

Natural Selections

Joseph Campana

UNIVERSITY OF IOWA PRESS

IOWA CITY

University of Iowa Press, Iowa City 52242
Copyright © 2012 by Joseph Campana
www.uiowapress.org
Printed in the United States of America
Design by Sara T. Sauers

The University of Iowa Press is a member of
Green Press Initiative and is committed to
preserving natural resources.

Printed on acid-free paper

A special thanks to Jane Mead, the 2011
Iowa Poetry Prize judge.

ISBN-13: 978-1-60938-081-6
ISBN-10: 1-60938-081-9
LCCN: 2011938430

for
Theodore Bale

I still, I still, I still

IT WAS AND IS to me still an important American place: northern and southern at the same time and eastern and Midwestern.—*James Wright*

Contents 🌿

1   Crow

2   Ohio 229

3   Natural Selections

8   Owl

9   Omen

10   Hare

11   Rural Morning

12   Fawn

13   Hunting the Beast

15   Kokosing

16   Creek

20   Kokosing

21   Homer, OH

26   Eagle

27   Ohio 308

28   Cardinal

29   Winesburg, OH

33   Crane

35   Finch

36   Sheltering Bough

37   Blue Heron

38   Wright

39   Jay

40 Democracy in Ohio

42 Sparrow

43 Bat

44 Rural Evening

48 Wolf

49 Spring Comes to Ohio

51 Ohio 661

52 Ladybug

53 Firefly

56 Snake

57 Rural Night

59 Crows

60 *March* (1939)

Acknowledgments ❧

GRACIOUS THANKS to those who read one of the (variously titled) versions of this book: Janet McAdams, Martha Collins, Paolo Asso, Paul Otremba, Katie Peterson, Ian Morse, Michelle Robinson, Amanda Moore, Stephen Burt, Susan Wood, and Louise Glück.

My colleagues at Kenyon College and Rice University have been generous, encouraging, and supportive throughout the process of writing and publishing this book. Many thanks.

Without my family and friends, where would I be? It is my good fortune that you are too many to name and your ill fortune that my thanks are too poor.

"Snake" is for Gordon Teskey. "Winesburg, OH" is for Nolan Marciniec. "Hunting the Beast" is for Brian Lee Morrison Jr.

Special thanks to the state of Ohio.

Grateful acknowledgment to the editors of the journals where versions of these poems first appeared: *American Letters & Commentary*: "Creek"; *Boston Review*: "Fawn"; *Cincinnati Review*: "Eagle"; *Colorado Review*: "Hare"; *Conjunctions*: "Crow," "Owl," "Cardinal," "Jay"; *Guernica*: "Omen"; *Gulf Coast*: "Wolf," "Crows"; *Kenyon Review*: "Sheltering Bough"; *Literary Imagination*: "Natural Selections"; *Prairie Schooner*: "Finch," "Ohio 661," "Rural Evening," "Sparrow"; *Slate*: "Spring Comes to Ohio"; *Subtropics*: "Ladybug"; *The Journal*: "Crane," "Wright."

Crow

Crow said *murder* and
then there was one. If

there were two, if
there were myriad

black wings covering
black winds beating sky.

Sky said *malice*. Crow
saw it shining. Glitter

of the needful, glitter
of the wanting ones:

dark hunger dark in
trees. Whither, crow,

now: who will you run to?

Crow said *murder*. And
then there were more.

And then there were more.

Afternoon hawk circles.
Another senseless road
ripped around a bend.
How potent the longing,
how potent the fear.
The two as one, the two
as hawk and shadow
comb a lifeless road.
Doesn't empty mean
safe? Another snap,
another twig, another
instinct ended. We
were all hungry,
circling each other's
flesh as if it were
nourishment. How
did the hawk know
what was left
on the side of this
road would spite
appetite, never end it?

Natural Selections

1.

Evidence that life invents
the conditions of survival
was visible, there, on those
roads. Driving away from
the center, away from
distraction: what is life
if not the index of what
waits to be desired?

2.

Leaving you was something
else entirely. And for what?
A little nowhere: a few hills,
islands of rarefied growth
isolated from the streams
of death and convergence
below. Driving back and
forth I could hear some
whisper of the new.
Everything was wrong.
The principle of evolution
is change, not growth.

3.

Nothing to do now.
Nothing but leave trees,
find streets of shoes and
the myriad satisfactions
of stores. In one a woman
identified our particular
species. When I said I
was a teacher, she sighed.
You probably have to teach
Darwin, don't you?
No, I said, *Shakespeare.*
Well, she said, warming
to her theme, *it's all*
the same in the end isn't it?

4.

Careless watcher
of dark thinking birds
without anywhere to
roost, climb to the top
of the sky, look down
and see everything:
how deeply small,
how slowly moving
without purpose or
origin or end. From
this distance you
can pretend you
are one of the sad,
one of the small
animals below.

5.

Tell me again how we were
at the top of the food chain,
how the climb to the leafy hilltop
made us believe it. This is not
to answer the question you
asked me. Nothing here
resembles an answer.

6.

When I arrived there were only
hand-wrought planks, work
of a banished carpenter, and
green light from the windows
creating the suggestion
of forest floor. It was,
I was told, an *old and storied
place* I was moving to, moving
away from you. At night I
could hear only myself and
the motions of unknown animals.
In the bookstore, the biography
of a great and suicidal poet. What
held the book together, the glue,
was so dried up, each page pulled
out as I read. *Not all of them,*
I thought in the dark, and in
the darkness, I wanted so much
to live I would have killed to live.

7.

Nothing is more complacent
than a house. Its secret,
in the end, is what is shared.

8.

Every so often I heard noise
without a body between the walls
of my kitchen and the world.
I tried not to think ill of
what I could not see and
remembered *there is nothing
either good or bad but thinking
makes it so*. This seemed
one of many exceptions.
Unable to sleep I listened to
its travels. Where could it go?
The house was so cold it made
no sense anything would stay
day after day, night after endless
night knowing at some moment
one of the tired animals would
falter while the other would
live on, awake and obsolete.

9.

Imagine there was no reason
to live as we did, in danger
of nothing at all. Imagine
there was something wrong
with being harmless. That it
was, in fact, a form of harm.
No, the house would whisper.
It was always a matter of survival.
The fittest were those with
the least to lose. I sat in
the center of a house that was
nowhere particular in Ohio,
in the world, in my life, missing you
so deeply someone might have
mistaken my song for the elusive
language of beasts and birds.

Owl

It's you, said the tree, and
the darkness said nothing.

Summer turned to snow
and still no answer.

It's you, said the sky, but
the darkness scarcely blinked.

Eyes opened wider and wider.
So the world began: it showed us

nothing. *It's you,* I said. And then:
I'm waiting. The night was so dark

and still so real. I was tiny, and
the trees tired. All was silence:

ravenous, unmoved.

Omen

Outside, and without warning,
the inexplicable raised its ugly
head. The temperature went,
again, and the sun went too:
all south. And wouldn't you
know a single dark crow was
sitting on a gravestone like
a vicious monument to patience,
mocking sleep, as if the world
needed more cheap significance.
All night through the woods
rain made the same sullen song
because the world had drunk
and drunk and drunk it in. All
the bottles are empty: all the
storm clouds have given up.
You are not yourself a form
of truth. You are drowning but
knowing so will not help you.

Hare

Hare says *Moon* but Moon
won't answer. Hare twitches.

Overhead darkness. Moon peers
down at the blues and greens:

scuffle, darken, fade, fade to black.
Everything's shutting down now.

Moon says *where am I?*

Hare rolls its eyes at circling
lights. Hare trembles. Even

the light will grow weary.
Moon all alone bleeds out

a reddish wake of grief. Moon
says *I never mean to leave you.*

Hare says *no.* Tremors from
the treacherous undergrowth.

Says, *I know I know I—no.*

Rural Morning

There's no irony in storm.
There's no irony in Ohio
as strong as the force
that binds torn petals
to the soaked porch.
What you wanted
from leaf, what you
wanted from tree
died in the night.
You could spend
all morning trying
to sweep them.
You could spend
all morning trying
to clean. Splintered
boughs blossom
in disguise, the scars
proof that you must
believe the trees.
You must believe
the last good drop
of honey dripped
from the lips
of a broken deer
hanging dead on
a branch above a creek
drying beneath the sun
only then to drink
its fill from the sky.

Fawn

What could be elegance is all instinct.
I am so tired of the fear around me

but I have no idea whose fear it is.
All I know is another roar and cry

another sweeping light and my legs
frozen fast now and something so

startling it must be good though I
know it cannot be anything but

another night black scurry, another
disaster waiting to seize, on the

dark roads, on the dark dark roads
it is so cold I could crouch down

here on the crackling leaves, and
let the black snow bleed over me.

Hunting the Beast

You're old enough to lie,
to grab the beast by its throat:
cock the rifle, grip the barrel,
jam the butt to your shoulder
so it hurts and loose the bullet
from its cavern of scorn, howling.

To know the beast, to know
the deer, to know an enemy
scuffling in undergrowth:
shudder of capture, now it's over.
Rabbits lie down in their warrens
but you will drive them forth.
Hawks twist in the clouds:
they will hide the sun.

You're old enough to know,
to be the bowstring ripped taut,
to stretch air into shape, to feel
the arrow explode into form and
catch in the haunch of a dark
forest, its flesh your nightmare.

To speak of anger, to speak of failure:
report of weapons, retort of trees,
taunt of wind. You want to trail the beast.
You know the paths of twisting wood
but you cannot track yourself.
The mind is full of sound, like the body.

You're old enough to kill, to drag
corpses in snow. This is how you
learn to see the world: the bird
hauled up with its dun plumage.
It is your hand alone that makes
the wings flutter, that squeezes
dream from the lungs of the dead.
If you can't fly away, no one will.

Kokosing

River gave up no
tokens of certainty.
The husk of its
revelation was
a body beyond
its own death.
All night, the deer
would not speak.
All winter it hung
from a tree over
water the color
of envy. As if it
required witness.
You are no hunter,
you, no purveyor
of dream. You can
do nothing for it.
Here comes spring:
the world blossoms
and blows away.
No one looks up
to see. No one
drags the deer
down from the tree.

Creek

*

I've seen in you that awful
need to tell: the way the water
slicked you back, all surfaces
now beyond resemblance.

*

To say a thing was frozen in
the tree or that it hauled its
dying bulk up the slickened
bark counter to sensible
recourse, for there was
nothing there: no leaf, no star.

*

The way the cold will break
the will. It will scatter. The
thousands pressed, the will
now everywhere dark and
cooling deep in soil. The body
was a test, and you failed it.

*

The condition of the river is
flux. So too the condition of
the beast that cannot sleep.
Imagine it crawled up into a
tree seeking dream. Imagine
ascent a form of prayer. The
end of all animals is stasis.
Birds bed down in bushes,
deer freeze to unfeeling bark.

*

If there is no motion there is
still motion of a body, a body
collapsing into little crevices,
into ever smaller mysteries. If
you listen closely, you can hear
the gradual shattering of the
branches under that weight.

*

Is it a ladder or a broken tree?

*

To stretch forth into, to hang,
entire, over a blighted scrap of
land because there is nowhere
else to run to, and the river
that was flood is now the
barest trickle. The tree is dry.
There's no reason to touch it.

*

How the sky tracks you. How
lines connect your stars.

*

There was a story of how you
came back. Slowly, at first,
stirring deep in the entrails
of the thing and then the dead
no longer dead, crawling forth
from a slickened gray body
first like a slug and then in
flight with such vicious, such
violent joy. You were always
changing. You said *nothing
was ever so sweet.* I could
hear the riddle bristling like
a miracle.

*

To be the tree broken by its
own heaviness. To be hanging
in a posture of determined
rupture: the lesson in question
was for the hands. They will
not be beside themselves.
Break now, hands. Break now
or reach out and be broken.

*

Were you lying there, were it
your breath escaping, visible,
wouldn't you want to be lifted
into someone's snaking arms?

*

Nothing left to be. The colors
were all cold, even as spring
limped back. There was such
silence in the world and it
would not let go. Why should
you stay, why should you hold
on unless you were waiting all
this time to billow back to life?

Kokosing

Everyone wants to be saved.
The finches just won't do it:
they don't even sing right.
Then, again, neither do you
wheezing along the river as
if you broke something
and waited to be punished.
The river fills with life
to spite you. How it stinks
before you, how it glistens
like dew on leaves, murky
air scented with the taint
of lightning. Look down:
what broke was you.
The only angels here
hang from sodden trees.

Homer, OH

Forty-nine miles from my
doorstep to the terminal in
Columbus. One quarter tank
of gas. Three small roadways,
no tolls, no time to stop.
Inevitable transit, from which
time seemed absent. I could
name my destination, or I
could name my love. There was
always rain, wind whipping ice
across steely roads. As I drove,
I counted the highway lights
because I knew they would
never run out.

*

Nor did most of the suitors
believe Penelope spent all
that time on a single tapestry.
Could she have been so
industrious as to finish each
night, a new one appearing
each bright morning? Might
she have been enjoying the
suitors in turn under cover of
night, each sworn to secrecy?

If the heart is made of flesh,
there is no way to say it breaks.
If it is made of blood, perhaps
it can only bleed. King Lear in
King Lear asks his own heart
to break. He asks because it
won't and he is a stubborn man.
What luxury to have a body
that breaks when the mind can
stand no more. The mind is
pure in and of itself. The heart
bleeds in the mind as the color
of the sun crashing into the
hills. I drove with the sky right
behind me, burning itself alive,
but never did I look back.

*

There was a secretary I knew
who lived in Homer but worked
in Ithaca. She spent her time
typing. We were no longer to
call her a secretary. She spent
her time driving as well:
twenty-six miles each way, each
mile a different letter, each trip
a useless expression of want,
each habitual transit another
sentence without end.

22

*

Ungrateful heart, love is far
away. Even were it near, it
would still be an imprecise
designation. Stop talking.
Someone could be waiting
for me. Stop looking at me:
someone must be holding his
heart out in his hands.

*

Homer never saw Ohio.
Still, he crossed the wooded
passageways from the towns
of New York to the edges of
an elaborately empty garden
only to find himself left alone
with houses sliding into creeks
and cars waiting on the lawn to
be taken for a ride. Of course,
Homer never did see anything.

*

The condition of waiting is the
string pulled so tight it might
bleed. If only the fates can spin
the threads and measure the
lengths woven between us, let

them make them longer, for
though I am not as far from
you as I might be, I feel the tug
of each mile, each numerable,
each vibrating with the hushed
roar of time passing over.

*

Ignominious, the fate of
names. There are nine towns
named Homer in the United
States, eleven if you include
Homerville. Homer was no
match for Arcadia (12), Aurora
(18), Athens (16). Troy (26) wins
hands down. Figures.

*

I try to imagine the settlers,
the makers of place, styling
themselves latter-day Adams,
scattering the names of gods
and poets, cities and heroes.
Did they allow themselves to
imagine Homer could tame the
trees or send game hurtling into
the hungry arms of the pioneers,
ripe for the kill? Why name me
an already forgotten dream?

*

Outside the car we pass several
towns in succession. Each is
named Homer and none of them
is home. Homer has one soda
machine. Now it feels as if a test
is about to begin. If the machine
is filled daily and a different,
desperate traveler passes by
each night with a thirst nothing
can quench, what could possibly
be left by morning?

*

There are no Homers in
America. I knew you anyway:
not by the scar, not by the
writhing trunk of the olive tree
we made our bed. Before I saw
your face I knew you, like a man
in midst of marathon, each mile
before and behind pulling like
a taut string. Like the man who
already knows whether he's
running from or running to.

Eagle

I'm blind, said the eyes, and
the eyes had it: the snow

was drifting down, the snow
wiping clean its dirty slate.

Overhead eagle swooped
and swooped without regard.

I'm wet cried the eyes while
the snow stretched for miles,

and there was nothing to see
above it, nothing below.

Above, eagle narrowed,
narrowed a pocket of sky.

Take me, said the eyes.
Eagle would not have it.

Ohio 308

Like the grim balloons
of an endless night sky
these crows hang over
into day and settle
in the bodies of trees.
Because you couldn't
stop for them, you
couldn't stop looking.
Downhill and past
two schools, a stone
church settles into dirt.
It is miserable to feed,
to be fed by the sky. Not
even the dense particulars
of everyday reverie keep
the mind from seeking
shelter above and away
from the tender carrion
fields where broken gods
drown in a trickling stream.

Cardinal

Spill or be spilled said the
law and the forest grew

and grew quiet: the quiet
was lasting. *If I had blood*

to spare, said the air, *it*
would already be spilling.

The air stopped short,
the earth trembled.

Had you any nerve you'd
have already stretched forth

to spill me. Then there would
be no one left to be singing

If I had hands I'd have
blood on my hands.

Winesburg, OH

Under the caress of his hands doubt
and disbelief went out of the minds of
the boys and they began also to dream.
—Sherwood Anderson

1.

In 1919 the story of my childhood
was written. It was set in Ohio.
I was none of the major characters.
Every story is a tale of grotesque
individuality. Decades later,
when I was born, I knew I'd be a poet
because I was afraid of my hands.

2.

Limbs are the extensions of man
and therefore also the sources
of dream. Imagine the clean-limbed
boys gathering under trees whose
branches, like hands that grasp,
hold up the sky. Each knot
is one of the infinitely numerable
beads of prayer. They can't
hold the sky up for very long.

3.

What needs a poet but hands
and what need hands but places
of hiding? The world is brutal,
which is why it is full of stories.

4.

The function of poetry is the memory
of touch. Is it then beautiful to feel
the same, to feel the familiar shame,
as if any shade of achievement was
like the touch of those articulate
hands which I wished were mine
and which I wished would hold
steady the world I wanted to touch.

5.

Speech was a theory of touch, its
practice excitation. I was born when
you spoke to me. I was born when
you wouldn't tell me your story.

6.

What is the body but what learns
in being touched? Is it that you
love your teachers or that all love
is love of first things, of the first

grasping of a world that will not
let you be? Did you love him?
Could his love for you hurt you?
Did you love anything not yourself?

7.

As if everyone had taken the same
bait offered by hands from the sky.
To think the words were confessions
of a personal nature and in the realm
of event. Each a different need
speaking through what vehicle,
what body was ready and apparent.
Perhaps not ready to be touched.
That once I saw you as the occasion
of my own memories. The years I
called that sight. To that singular
question asked. The answer yes.

8.

In 1974 began the story of touch.
The story lasted as long as the dream.
As for stories that are awful and true.
As for the desire to reach forth and
to understand everyone as what must
be grasped. As for hills, the memory
of hills, or some original imagined
contact. Those who touch us first
are those from whom we never part.

9.

Easy to say there's nothing here.
These are not your dead, these
are not your beloved. If you knew
how to look at these hills, you'd see
the earth buck, sway like a sea of hands.

Crane

In Akron, in the brutal streets
of Akron with the words, with
all those damnable words and
a bastard of a father, mother
upstairs, idle, thinking of stores
the smell of stores and candy
with the gold foil wrapping and
unwrapping. How vulnerable
sweet things are in the light, in
the wretched day when nothing
ever was so sweet or just couldn't
stay sweet long. Every town you
know is like every word known:
souring open in Cleveland, in
Cleveland in the mansions of
luxury, which really is a kind of
lust as is the will to be ill on the
edge of a lake of liquid fire when
the sun burns across every wish
you ever had, and they are ripping
up the sky each morning, in the
awful morning. The bed is still
empty and the page even whiter
than the day before because words
are eating up the mind (and there
is nowhere to go but in and out
of the mind) and so does work,
so does work devour the mind

with its terrible twisting of hands.
There's no help in warehouses:
everything is full, everything waits
to be sorted, to be sold, to be wanted
and no one really knows how to be
wanted in daylight, under the strictures
of light, or deep in clandestine night
with the hungers and the men all
awful and sweet and almost invisible.
This is not your America, you think,
only it is. This is not your smell, only
it is. You won't go back, only you will.
Why not call the street what it really is?

Finch

Everything costs

some thing, some
time, some one.

One is surely
the number of beauty:

every flicker of wing
is a whip. If beauty

reigns it reigns over
the broken. The gold

is for falling, is for
brutalities you hope

won't tarnish.
The gold is for

quickening, is for
never lifting above.

Sheltering Bough

Shelter won't come from the sky:
look how the trees sway to stand.
But they never let you down, and
in the dream so closely mirroring
this night, storms would hush
the world clean and darken lights
that pain the eye and having passed
leave only the sounds of water
collecting, as if the earth, so bursting
with bloom, hungered for a sweet
and endless deluge. As you bring
yourself to pray for this, you can't
find your hands. Bring on the night
with its silken torpor. Bring down
the moon from her icy perch. She is
too relentless and holds all the trees
in place. And as for those of lunar
temperament, for those for whom
habitation is transit, like blue heron
huddled by the riverbank, they are
the ones who build, the ones who haunt,
the ones looking for a place to leave.

Blue Heron

To grasp water,
to find sky
pierced
by the eye
of a heron
haunting shore:
cold and sweet
as endless sleep.

Wright

He held acquaintance with waves
when there was no water and the
trees so dry they would hold no
one above the carnage that was
everywhere so ordinary no one
could see it. He held acquaintance
with waves when there was no water
to walk on and the withering stalks
so deep anything might sink but
nothing would rise up again. He
rode waves of devastation, what
you call expectation: so human,
so likely to fail, to raze, to rend,
to tear sweet marrow from land
from which little could be made.
He held acquaintance with a will
to look up from the wasted, ignorant
bloom of a nightmare born in the
unclean waters of memory. He held
acquaintance with nightmare: he held
it in his hand. The holding was a kind
of love. No one wanted to touch it,
this land. He held it up to the sky,
held acquaintance with a sky clean
and undeserved. He held it, and he
suffered it. He held it up and sang.

Jay

Don't be blue, said the sky,
but the world wouldn't

listen. Each night tasted
like drowning, each day

choked on its own bloom.
There were darker things

than the eye of sky, there
were smaller things too.

Don't be said the blue
so the light stole away.

As for the twisted leaves?
As for the idols of morning?

Nothing left to be.
Nothing left to know.

Democracy in Ohio

November 2, 2004

What wouldn't you stand for if you would
stand nine hours waiting to have conferred
on you the rights that render your animal

flesh less vulnerable to herding or culling?
And shouldn't there be something to save
you from being thrust into a landscape not

of your own choosing? I've seen you before.
You are like me, no more than a hackneyed
imitation of a creature capable of want.

On the sides of dark roads you count deer
reduced from a state of will to mere statuary.
No need to forage, no need to feed. They can

be counted on not to speak. Injustice, injustice:
it is not a matter of right. It is a matter of hunger,
of the all-consuming hunger for retribution

that sends a car, almost of its own accord,
to a road at night populated by such grim
and unreal specters. Don't count on spring,

don't count on being counted. Everything
can be taken, even the roads can be taken
away. Say you stood nine hours, winding

through public space, an old school now
the barren seat of the smallest instance of
government, with a determination born of

futility. Is this what it is to be governed not
by the kingdom of animals? It is not your
right to choose between just and unjust.

It is your right to fill with rage the way
the night fills with the sounds of what
animals here do best: feed and die.

We were all lost on the same sad route
with the moon above us burning down
as if nothing had happened and no one had

been rendered an unseen consequence. Tell me
something real. Tell me this road isn't really
an unending scream. When will spring come?

I feel closer now to being a stone than before,
which is why, here in this place, I started to sing.

Sparrow

Sun says *sing*. Bird
doesn't want to.

Snowdrops bursting
bursting up to die.

Sun says *open*.
Bird won't do it.

Chill wind combing,
combing through

the dead. Sun says
linger. Bird isn't

listening. Wings
beat harder, harder

now to die. Sun
sings *providence*.

And the bird
says *fall*.

Bat

All flesh wants is a little
food, a little sleep. It does

not want to know what is
before it or what it already

knows as darkness. To live
as flesh is to live on sound

for it is, at last, all feeling.
So everything ends, and it

ends with a precipitous sweep
of wings, a singular buffet

of wind, and a tiny scream.

Rural Evening

Nature isn't cruel it just
doesn't know when to quit.
Neither did hundreds of
workers at the Rolls Royce
plant in Mount Vernon, so
the company did it for them,
gradually, so the gesture would
be sad and necessary and
complete, like the reluctant
setting of the sun in another
string of inevitable evenings.
Such kindness we're to think of
this evening, on the porch, not
idle hands left to the piecework
of despair. But that is not what
this poem is about. Outside,
the grass won't quit either.
No one ever taught it not
to keep thrusting up and
weaving broken vessels
in the dirt, just as no one told
the stray cat not to have kittens
in a bush next to a dirty garage.
Nor did anyone tell the kittens
not to hide under the porch
or that they could drink milk
provided for them even if
they were afraid of the man

who left it. If I am that man,
do I wonder, tonight, what's
the use of kindness when
every attempt at auspicious
action spills milk on the porch
and feeds no one? And what's
this poem about? Ask those
workers fired in lines three
through eleven if they had
any intention of being drafted
into a poem when poetry is made
to speak for no one. Still, it wasn't
the poet who sent them packing
to sell twelve kinds of nothing
any hour of the day or night.
Picture the poem as a factory:
in goes suffering and out come
words, when all the kittens wanted
was sustenance. They had shelter
under a porch I wouldn't know
how to fix. The rotting porch
will still creak when the kittens
flee or prove less fit
than other hungers. Nature
isn't cruel it just can't stop
making complications, which we
often call pain. Take the man
in Columbus crying *innocent*
and the woman crying *justice*.
In between, the body of a dead
child found by fishermen.
Picture the poem as whatever

you can: monster, murderer,
bystander, hero. Picture the
mother an avenging fury and
the poem as a prisoner you
want to believe whether he's
lying or not. Notice I didn't
mention what I want to believe.
When I said "body" earlier I
meant "skull." Picture the poem
as a long series of pleas because
no one stops making those.
Nothing is certain except
the actual fact of crime. I
couldn't tell you about that
or about the type of blue bird
skulking in the oak out front.
The kittens, they seem to have
gone. Did someone love them,
did someone fear for them,
did someone drag their bodies
from beneath the porch and
haul them into the air no more
than objects of some misguided
care? That is to say, did I?
The moon above tonight
is auspicious, and I'm told
it can remember the birth
of a prophet who understood
how we suffered, how we
couldn't stop suffering, even
when nothing was wrong
especially when nothing was

wrong and how for all our
real and insignificant pain we
observe death but can't feel
for others creaturely affiliation.
It's easier with kittens, no?
You can hold them in one
hand, and, if you had to, you
could squeeze. So I tried,
spirit of unattached pain,
to feel love for the world,
and to touch its creatures
with kindness. I was tired,
almost too tired to bring
the bowl of milk inside and
leave it with others waiting
to be scraped out and spilled
over the earth like a gift,
like the shining freight of
an indifferently spinning
wheel. I closed the door,
and finally I was ready
for the silence that followed.

Wolf

Little man, I said, keep the wolf
from my door: one more night,

one more wretched night and day.
The wolf said *wait* and the season

was packing its bags, but it would
not leave and it would never leave.

Little man, I said, there's a tooth
at my throat, and the tooth said

time and it was really a wolf and it
was cloaked in a sheep's skin of

satisfaction, and there was a fury
raining down at night and it tapped

at the windows. Little man, I said,
close the door, there's a wolf in

the air, and there is a fury that even
fear can't touch and it is gnawing

me, I feel it gnawing at me and
the wolf said *shelter* and I knew it

was a lie, I felt it as a lie, I could
already feel its teeth tearing my skin.

Spring Comes to Ohio

The first gesture is despair
because the snowdrops
have fled and the cold
came back anyway. You
are far from your love
and you will be nothing
but the space between
the hand and what it is
accustomed to grasping.
The first gesture is cold
but the rain still comes
down and like the rain
you lean your head down
on someone's shoulder
because it is too heavy for
you to carry by yourself.
Outside the boys are like
flowers and the flowers
like boys because they
don't give what they say.
All the evening flowers
are coffins bursting with
possibility. Why not pick
one, why not let your
sorrow sink into the dirt
where it will die? The first
gesture is the hope that it
will die before you will
or that you will learn to

read it like a book. Come
read, come to the flower
beds and the mowed-down
fields where the heads of
yellow soldiers burst in
the grass. If anyone ever
gave you something, that
gesture of fading beauty
was the first sign that
the price of generosity
is the flower that would
rather not be ripped from
its heart. Come read all
the flowers: they were
printed here just for you.
Come read your heart,
which has shriveled
into a flower receding
before night. If the sun
ever will come back,
the first thing you'll do is
reach right out to touch it.

Ohio 661

I haven't a coin in my pocket to spare
and it is powerfully dark outside my
window tonight. Because I've been
driving for hours past almost nothing,
the roads are far too modest for lights
or houses. And though I am a stranger,
passing swiftly through, I know these
roads, the way they insist upon night
because you cannot see pain in the dark.
All you can see are the painted wonders,
soda machines oracular and insistent:
they are the only beacons around.
And if you had some quarters or
some courage, you'd pull yourself
over even if what beckons is not
your home, will not be your home.
The roads would strangle you,
so you just don't stop, you will
not stop, but you will not break
down and pray to any other light.

Ladybug

What is
a promise
but what is
delicate,
prone
to flight?

Firefly

1.

Don't go out on me something said. It
was almost too small to be perceived.

The world was dizzy from pain.
Like the voice, it came from nowhere.

2.

Follow, trace the fading light
into the woods, into the water.

The bank struggles to hold flood
the way a body struggles to retain

life: both in utter darkness.

3.

So the hero flew to the moon,
as they do in stories, to face

her unyielding cycle of return.
Did he steal from her shadowy

wake a secret to send
the furious world to sleep?

Tell me softly. I am already
drifting beneath silvery waters.

4.

Heroes disappear. All the time.
When they return, they're never

the same. So you see, my love
was always a form of myth.

I tried to tell you this as many
times as a firefly sends its

delicate code to lights too
far above ever to reply.

5.

Shouldn't the night win, I said,
shouldn't it win its tireless wager?

No you said. What do you see,
in the sky, but countless bodies

ripping themselves into light?

6.

There is a body whose sole task
is to communicate in a language

easily mistaken for joy. It is not
a code flickering. You can't read it.

Look, now it's daytime. Look, now it's night.
It's the same each time because you are.

Snake

Always a song sliding
under a porch

always a tooth dragging
stars around dirt:

skin is not for air
skin is not for water.

Something wants a voice
in dark places.

Something wants
to curl around

the whirling earth.

Rural Night

Like the sullen sliver
of a bruised eye
this moon shines
only over Ohio:
who else would
want it? Almost
everyone dreams
as long rains
sweep the fields
clean. You could
sit for hours
laboring in night
to watch as another
quiet hour devours
the insistent
rustling of leaves,
the cries of bats
scraping the eaves.
See how the
rhododendrons
sag under dripping
trees: it is sadness
to drown in sleep.
Anything could
happen at night
but nothing will.
The one who
dreams is never

the one who leaves.
Look at the torn sky:
if the moon sends
you to sleep forever
is that how you
know it loves you?

Crows

The boys are hungry
the boys are circling

the boys are singing
their anthem in the dark

where there is no shame:

*there is not enough
there's never enough.*

The road shines tonight
to blind all the stars

and the floor lights up
a storm of painted eyes:

the boys watch closely
the boys will fluster.

It is the same furious
dance over and again.

The boys don't mind
the boys won't cry

and if they're crying
they're crying *more.*

March (1939)

Grant Wood's Iowa not—what

    did you call it?—*my Ohio.*

Nothing mine about it, especially not

    those creatures scurrying, resentfully

alive, on the sides of snaking roads and somehow

    more unsettling than the remnant dead.

For two years I try not to have anything.

    Instead, I imagine Grant Wood in Paris.

How unlikely the time a certain kind

    of American spends in Europe,

wondering what exactly he is. I suppose

    for some it doesn't matter:

anywhere but home *is* home, which is how

    I thought of myself. Not so. Not so

for Grant Wood, hopelessly American and in

    the dark middle of the nation from which

no traveler returns. Picture him ensconced at home,

    his bitter family crowded around to watch

him at a favorite pursuit: *tableaux vivants.*

Wood reclines, Wood supplicates, Wood reaches

up to a wordless heaven.

I know that stillness

from his cartoon swells of hill and field.

Picture him a latter-day Antigone,

able to speak but unwilling. There is

something in his paintings

of the burden of what he could never say.

Sometimes the only choice is

to be buried alive. *My Ohio.* I say it over

and over again. In the corner of the window,

on the corner of a street in Mount Vernon,

the glassy eye of the stag stares at no one.

You can see that particular look

in the eyes of men buried alive by longing.

Are they not everywhere around here,

nearly turned to stone by their own

reluctance? I know those men, casting about like

wolves afraid of their own teeth.

Something about the sky says,

    Take this land. In the end, the land wins.

What heaven, Grant Wood, were you

    looking for that you could not find

in crooked stiles puncturing the soil

    along the broken roads of America?

You wanted to love it, but you couldn't understand

    the shame was a form of love.

It is dark here, especially tonight,

    and far too quiet. I cannot stay

any longer waiting for you. But I will

    follow the road you've left,

to the house on the hill in the dream of the sky,

    and I will wait for the stars to swing open a door.

Iowa Poetry Prize & Edwin Ford Piper Poetry Award Winners

1987
Elton Glaser, *Tropical Depressions*
Michael Pettit, *Cardinal Points*

1988
Bill Knott, *Outremer*
Mary Ruefle, *The Adamant*

1989
Conrad Hilberry, *Sorting the Smoke*
Terese Svoboda, *Laughing Africa*

1990
Philip Dacey, *Night Shift at the Crucifix Factory*
Lynda Hull, *Star Ledger*

1991
Greg Pape, *Sunflower Facing the Sun*
Walter Pavlich, *Running near the End of the World*

1992
Lola Haskins, *Hunger*
Katherine Soniat, *A Shared Life*

1993
Tom Andrews, *The Hemophiliac's Motorcycle*
Michael Heffernan, *Love's Answer*
John Wood, *In Primary Light*

1994
James McKean, *Tree of Heaven*
Bin Ramke, *Massacre of the Innocents*
Ed Roberson, *Voices Cast Out to Talk Us In*

1995
Ralph Burns, *Swamp Candles*
Maureen Seaton, *Furious Cooking*

1996
Pamela Alexander, *Inland*
Gary Gildner, *The Bunker in the Parsley Fields*
John Wood, *The Gates of the Elect Kingdom*

1997
Brendan Galvin, *Hotel Malabar*
Leslie Ullman, *Slow Work through Sand*

1998
Kathleen Peirce, *The Oval Hour*
Bin Ramke, *Wake*
Cole Swensen, *Try*

1999
Larissa Szporluk, *Isolato*
Liz Waldner, *A Point Is That Which Has No Part*

2000
Mary Leader, *The Penultimate Suitor*

2001
Joanna Goodman, *Trace of One*
Karen Volkman, *Spar*

2002
Lesle Lewis, *Small Boat*
Peter Jay Shippy, *Thieves' Latin*

2003
Michele Glazer, *Aggregate of Disturbances*
Dainis Hazners, *(some of) The Adventures of Carlyle,*
My Imaginary Friend

2004
Megan Johnson, *The Waiting*
Susan Wheeler, *Ledger*

2005
Emily Rosko, *Raw Goods Inventory*
Joshua Marie Wilkinson, *Lug Your Careless Body out*
of the Careful Dusk

2006
Elizabeth Hughey, *Sunday Houses the Sunday House*
Sarah Vap, *American Spikenard*

2008
Andrew Michael Roberts, *something has to happen next*
Zach Savich, *Full Catastrophe Living*

2009
Samuel Amadon, *Like a Sea*
Molly Brodak, *A Little Middle of the Night*

2010
Julie Hanson, *Unbeknownst*
L. S. Klatt, *Cloud of Ink*

2011
Joseph Campana, *Natural Selections*
Kerri Webster, *Grand & Arsenal*